A Tapestry OF Poetry

Woven by members of the
Suffolk Writers Group

SWG

Little Bear Publications

www.littlebearpublications.co.uk

ISBN 978-1-9161281-9-4

Designed and illustrated by Caryn Noad
www.carynnoadart.com

*Printed and bound in the UK
by Speedprint
www.speedprint.co.uk*

Sewn In Suffolk

These poems showcase the work of some forty members of
The Suffolk Writers Group and for most, this will be the first time
they would have seen their work in print.

In any poetic anthology you can expect a plethora of differing
styles and rhythms. No specific topic was given to the members
when they were invited to submit their poems, so in here you'll
find the styles and rhythms of them, as varied as the subject
matters themselves.

I'd like to thank Mai Black, founder of SWG, for her enthusiasm
for the project, and Caryn Noad for her creative input. I'd also like
to thank the members of SWG for their encouragement and of
course for submitting their wonderful work.

Gary Milsom
Little Bear Publications

Simply an
Ultra
Fantastic and
Friendly
Organisation of
Local and
Knowledgeable

Wordsmiths who
Rally together
Intent on composing
Tremendously
Epic works and
Readily offer
Support

Gaining such
Reviews and
Observations is
Ultimately
Priceless

Beverley Bowry

CONTENTS

CONTENTS

CONTENTS

CONTENTS

OF Philosophy & Life...

CONTENTS

Threads of Suffolk Writers thoughts silent unassigned - A paper stage their Aida cloth where they're sewn in line by line- Given voice and given rhythm so they dance and intertwine - And weave about their paper stage in a tapestry of rhyme.

SWG

Of Animals and Nature and Love

Tree of Life

For I cannot eat soil
nor take my energy from the sun
nor breath air that's not been sanitised
like you have since time on Earth begun
Neither can I easily
like animal and thee
live reciprocal relationships
In nature's harmony

But I eat the fruits you offer
breath the air you purify
and can reason think and understand
so embrace the reason why
without your presence in this world
I would surely die
you're the essence of existence
and I the passer-by

Gary Milsom
From Into The Woods
A collaboration with treescape artist
Debbie Baxter

Elegy to My Horse Dandy

Did the wind teach you to run so wild
Scattering bruised leaves in fields and woodlands?
The earth still trembles where you now lie
So I ask the question with no reply
I found you sleeping late that night
So still, head bowed, legs folded tight
Gone forever from my life, I'll always ask
What was your secret, Dandy?

Susan Penelope Sadler

A Rivers Tale

Can you hear in the distance
choirs singing their song?
Of bells that peel a winter's tale
whilst cattle move along

Icy rivers cut their path
through land to meet the sea.
Moving towards the dark abyss
of crashing waves
and thunderous clouds

Shards of light that spear the depths
both day and night.
It subsides to calmer places
it slows its ebb and flow
finding a passage,
a ditch, a bow.

Stretching its arms to reach
a field of frost and snow
a carpet laid by mother nature
protecting all that grows below.
Its icy fingers stretch beyond,
passing by the church
where jubilant folk ring their bells.
and children go in search.

Robins sit on snowy graves
and pretty layered birch.
Footsteps crunched on virgin snow
lay a wreath and say,
" We miss you oh so very much,
why did you go away?"
A tear rolls from eye to cheek
and drops upon the ground
Will it find you?
You hear nothing,
not a sound.

You'll not be found in the hard, cold ground;
your soul has moved above
to feel the breeze on rustling leaves
and see the spiky holly.
Twists of ivy on the walls
grow ever higher
to reach the heavens up above
way beyond the spire.

Can you hear the distant voices
of choirs that sing their song?
Of bells that peel a winter's tale,
the story will move on.

Belinda Rose Bond

My Little White Chair

My little white chair
calls me into the garden.
On fresh Spring days
the sun's broken rays
fall on the new buds that will open.

My little white chair
calls me into the garden.
On hot Summer days
I watch the birds play.
They sing as if to say
they have spoken.

My little white chair
calls me into the garden.
On cold Autumn days
all the colours ablaze
remind me of our soldiers fallen.

My little white chair
calls me into the garden.
On chilly Winter days,
snowdrops on display
give me hope for new growth
next new season.

Christine Cacot

The Network of Nature

Stretched out beneath the olive trees
I felt the breeze
illumination of the night
I saw moonlight
Eyes closed, the feeling to prolong
I heard birdsong
The breeze brought odours gently blown
I smelt pinecones
A gift arrived from woodland fairies
I tasted berries
Senses soaring and expressing Nature's blessing.

Susan Penelope Sadler

19

The Seasons of Life

I am the autumn;
maroon, swirling leaves
tussled by the breeze;
crinkled, decaying, underfoot,
hidden, awaiting spring.
I am the winter;
bitter, bright sunlight
that sparkles on the leaf;
crystal drops glistening
with the purity of death.
I am the spring;
new beginnings bud,
pushing through the detritus of decay;
a rebirth of life,
an innocence reborn.
I am the summer;
a blanket of warmth
that wraps my soul
in happiness.

Julie Missen

November in New Caledonia

Numerous people flock to the
Ocean shore to
View the
Evening sunlight with clouds
Merging to create a stunningly
Beautiful sunset which then
Evolves into a myriad of soft, velvet
colours called the
Rainbow of the night.

Christine Cacot

The Shape of Clouds

The shapes of clouds are numerous
parading through our skies
they conjure up imagination
in lots of children's eyes

Great shapes of wonder, fascination
forms with every view
massive cloudy atlases
to behold for me and you

They have such starry Latin names
some of which we know
their form determine likelihood
for storm or rain or snow

The stratus cloud hangs low and lifeless
greyish in its hue
it's flat and often featureless
with not a lot to do

The cumulus it changes form
and conjures up such sights
when children see strange animals
or Butterflies or kites

Cirrus is the delicate cloud
all feathery and light
largely made of crystal ice
in wispy shades of white

Towering cumulonimbus
like great mountains in the sky
haunt the low and middle atmosphere
that's seen with naked eye

Nimbostratus menacing
dark grey to block the Sun
bring arcus clouds before the storm
that roll in one by one

Cumulus congestus stand
like chimneys in our views
and lenticulus form spacecraft shapes
that crop up on the news

When we take the aeroplane
and breakthrough to the sky
we pass through cirrostratus veil
like cloud that hangs so high

Whatever shape and fancy name
a cloud has day to day
We are fascinated, awestruck
by their marvellous display

And when my time is done here
and through the gates I am allowed
I might just be that Butterfly
you see upon my cloud

Stephen Oakes

Two For Joy

A bird of stunning black and white
flashes past your view
Your heart leaps and you look about
hoping there'll be two
Or three or four or even more
Oh superstitious you
Good morning Mister Magpie
See I'm saluting you.

Gary Milsom
From Into The Woods
A collaboration with treescape artist
Debbie Baxter

You Have Power But I Have More

You can try your best,
To destroy my rest.
You have power but I have more.

You brought your men, and vicious machines.
You started your build through this mighty land,
destroying trees and souls.

This Amazonian land belongs to only me.
A force of nature you intend to destroy.
Your greed is morally blind.
Your efforts will be undone.

I willed the thunderous rains and let loose my reins.
Once they waned, your men complained.
No trace of their build or machines remained.

I devoured and destroyed it all,
your efforts undone,
You have power but I have MORE

Lina Hogg

Maisie

Why do I dedicate so much time to you
for so little in return?
Dark and refined, you remain aloof and remote.
I cherish the warmth
of your body, nuzzling close against me
like a hot water bottle in the night.
Only on your terms when the fancy takes you
am I the last resort,
You visit me when you decide.
I hear you tramping and
plodding upstairs not caring for my being.
Indifferent to my calls when I need
the comfort of your presence.
But if you need love you take it at your whim.
Finally an appearance,
your white socks softly strutting towards me.
Deciding at last to demand my attention.
You leap onto my lap
rubbing your head against my chin.
Purring in my ear you knead my leg.
Settling down, I scratch your ears.
Finally resting relaxed and content.

Christopher P. Stapleton

Untied

The darkly purple lavender stems
spring and quiver to the touch of
heavy bees, pestering the violet, hunting the nectar.
A combine in a distant field adds a ground bass
to the wood pigeons rhyming calls.
The songbirds silenced in the three o'clock heat.

Thyme moves slowly in a waft of cooler air
that lilts a potpourri of herbs and roses
caressing my skin.
Somewhere a clang that might be an ancient bell
mixes with the incessant insects' busy hover.
New growth on the manicured box is a livid yellow
Set against the deeper shades of last year's growth.

A heavy peace enfolds the knot garden.

Ian Hartley

27

What is a Garden

It can be a rolling lawn
to ride a sit on mower upon

A yard of paving stones with
pots of pansies and petunias

A place to sip your first cuppa of the day
while listening to the birds singing you
a merry morning as they play

A haven of memories of times gone by
an apple tree that once grew bananas magically
to make the grandkids eyes grow wide with wonder

Some shade upon a hot and sunny day
green leaves to cool your fevered brow,
breeze blowing fan like leaves to relieve
your troubled mind somehow

It can be your heart's delight
if messy country cottage
or ordered borders, straight and true
your garden reflects the truth of you

Public gardens for the masses to enjoy
looked after by busy workers full of care
to spread a carpet of sweet air
and colours many hued to give
many a mind some calm
and act as a hush point
to quieten noise and be a balm

Your garden is yours and mine is mine
Big or small on window sill
or by a roadside sign
All pleasure and life contained
within the contours of a small green leaf

Scent and sight, light, rain and sun
joy and peace, hard work and fun
a garden brings each of these and more
nature's bounty, plants, weeds and all
a tree can make us feel so small
a humble daisy makes giants of us all

Janet Dunn

The Mustang

Run, proud Mustang, nose to the wind
Your mane and tail flowing like silk
Wild eyed, with nostrils flared.

Hear the thunder of your hooves
Echoing across scorched plains
Freedom runs at your side

Nothing can hold you back
Man's laws mean nothing to you
No fence can contain you
Pioneer Spirit of the West
Once despised, today admired
Now roam the hills in peace.

Susan Penelope Sadler

The Wet Wind Sings

The wet wind sings,
Wake!
Water runs trickling in rivulets
penetrating oilskin, finding flesh
as peat paths are trudged through burnt bracken
dead heather impeding
grouse gorse snagging.
Stop, here's a little feather, speckled cream and brown.
Surface sparkling with raindrops.
Wake, look, see –
No need for sunsets or bright fields.

Ian Hartley

A Passage to India

They both drew rein, to grant the cobra space
To slither off into some apple trees,
Then cantered on, and urged their mounts to race
For all their worth. And yet their own unease
Was echoed in the thunder of the hooves;
The very earth said: "No – the cobra kills".
They heard it from the birds, the temple roofs,
The palaces, and from the distant, purple hills.
As fleetingly as they had nearly touched,
Instinctively their horses swerved apart;
The riders veered away, and tightly clutched
Both reins and hopes into their pounding hearts...
Resoundingly, from its own parapet,
The great, all-seeing sky cried "No – not yet".

Richard Spencer

English Apple Tree

There's something very English
about an apple tree
in a rustic garden
of a cottage by the sea
its gnarled black winter branches
wearing fur of green algae
looking old before its time
sleeping crookedly

There's something very English
about an apple tree
when it wakes up in the springtime
sprouting blossom fragrantly
a sweet delight of pink and white
for butterfly and bee
a lining for its summer coat
dark green and shimmery

There's something very English
about an apple tree
in early Autumn sunshine
with its fruit of red and green
round suspended clusters like
baubles on a Christmas tree
from now til mid-December yum
apple crumble for my tea.

Gary Milsom

In Blossom Time

Two sounds awake me: first, a drowsy bee
Caught in the curtains- then you calling me.

I feel your touch, your warm breath in my ear-
But reaching out, my fingers close on air-

Elusively, it seems, you've slipped away-
Beneath the cherry tree, where once we lay.

Loving the sudden sun, your chest is bare-
With easy grace, you bask in mellow air.

The fragile cherry blossom's shining white-
And glowing, round you pools a golden light.

"I'm here!" : but then a soaring sky-lark flies,
Pouring liquid music from the skies.

Upward we gaze- I turn to your loved face-
But you have vanished- in your empty place,

The skylark carolling, the dappled tree,
With snow of falling petals, floating free.

Catherine Guillemin
Previously published in The Oldie Magazine, April 2020
and poetrywivenhoe, day 208, 2023

The Sea at Night

The hypnotic sound
of these gentle seas
whispers, lovingly
to all that will hear,
clarifies, the lungs
of all that will breathe
in, the fresh air;
that takes us away
to far off lands
where our minds drift away.
The glint of the worlds window
reflects a thousand lost souls
onto, the softly lapping shadows
that caress our shores;
the shores of our minds
that take us away,
to far away places
where our dreams will stay.

Julie Missen

Early Autumn

The mist lifts and the dew glistens in the sunlight.
Not a cloud in the sky, promise of a glorious day.
A slight breeze gently caresses my cheek
and the trees sway to say good morning.
I sit on the wet lush grass,
clothes soaking up nature and nothing matters.
Only a quiet rustle of the leaves and
distant sound of early birds can be heard.
All is well in my world.
This is when I am connected to the spirit world-
above and below-
I feel whole and at peace.
The leaves are starting to turn yellow, red, and brown.
They cover the forest floor
and crunch as I walk so frighten a rabbit
and then a scurrying sound.
A flock of geese honk as they migrate to warmer climes
and I wave them goodbye.
"Have a safe journey, goodbye." I shout.

Lina Hogg

The Day the Goose Got Loose

I remember the day the goose got loose
Charging about like an angry moose
Only pausing to snap at the postman's boots
The farmer's face turned a shade of puce

The farmer thought the goose obtuse
And couldn't understand why he'd want to vamoose
Filling the farmyard with honks and hoots
That crazy goose was dangeroose!

By the afternoon they'd reached a truce
Both agreed they could be brutes
So, farmer Ted, and Bruce the goose
Deciding that all points were moot
And needing no further excuse
Made up over cake and juice

James Domestic

OF Comfort, Loss, and Well-being

Good Grief

Grief, when it catches you
young, old, tender, or bold
... can eat you up
It strikes like an arrow
in your heart
It creeps and seeps
to every corner of your being
without you seeing
It settles - beds-in
Then cries out
Long after you think it has passed

Like a strong wave, or a harsh wind
Grief feels cruel when it hits you
It can hijack the sweetest moments
and flood you
Again, and again
So, we must draw a circle
that includes
and accepts this pain
as a part of life
The loss of one loved deeply
and missed permanently
We can make peace with grief
Respect it
and give in
Not fight it
and stifle it
until it BURSTS
But love, and understand it.

Recognise the presence
of those not really lost,
but tapping on our hearts
our minds
our memories.
For our grief is our loved ones
nestled in our beating hearts
when we're apart.

There ... there.
Whispering their love
their reminder
you are still with them
and they are with you
But for now -
simply elsewhere

Jane Spencer-Rolfe

Growing Home

There's a knot in my chest
Where you've left me stunned
Like a rabbit
Frozen in the road

Where you question my growth
Like you think you know
When it is all
I've ever known

There's a hole in my lung
Where I'm short of breath
Like a fox,
from the hound, on the run

Where you question my voice
And my right to speak truth
When being silenced
Is all I have known

But there's room in my soul
Where each time I've loved
And walked when
I know my worth

For a rainforest to flourish
For my heart to nourish
Oxygen regeneration
Rebirth

I'll decide,
what growth looks like for me
And when and what I can speak
I'll judge my intentions
And integrity
And make sure history is not on repeat

Why would I trust
the opinion of a person,
who never truly loved me
Only an impossible,
non-existent, type,
a fantasy kind of somebody

One he's designed
In his mind
To fit his idea
Of perfection

One he'll coerce
And control
In the guise of
Respect and loving protection

There's a knot in my chest
Where you've left me stunned
Like a rabbit
Frozen in the road

But these blinding headlights
I've seen before
I know
How to get myself home

I know to sit still
And let it all pass
Because nothing will
Crush what I've grown

Then I'll run with the wild
And play with the fae
With love like a child
And free to the bone

Sylvie Songbird

Mum's Resting Place

Today I see the questionable greyness
of unspoken clouds
as the tepid sun drips with distracting delight
and languid angel waves are somersaulting
cartwheels of salty air

A lone Red Admiral sketches
a place between sand and sea
wings sign-posting the burial haven
where in seven days we will bury mum's ashes

The sand will open its vast body to absorb
fragments of volcanic love trickling
as the purple tide of prayer dances mum home

Sarah Caddick

Lee's Poem

Walk my rods down to the beach
and cast a lead for me
watch the leads flight, hear the reel sing
at the place I love to be

Take your stance with hands apart
twist to bend the rod's back
turn and launch the lead so high
the heavens feel its crack

My initials stamped upon its base
show my help in its design,
prove its veracity take your cast
make your reels whine

It's sad you'll see me cast no more
no rods or reels for me,
just know I will be watching from above
as you stand beside the sea

For me my match is over
I've walked off from my peg,
But remember that my love goes on
no more has to be said

Fred Fish
In memory of Lee Graham Adams
28th Aug 1982 to 26th Sept 2022

Broken Window

I see your face through
the cracks of a broken windowpane
Your jagged eyes dance
across the splintered frame
That crooked smile turns away
from my guessing gaze.
Impossible to know you.

I watch your silhouette slip
into the blurry lines of dusk
Your shadow fades
but I can still see you; just.
I scream an old song of longing
that you will not touch.
Impossible to hear you.

The sun falls silently from
the sky's fragile hold.
Like a weary penny dropping.
Unheard. Untold.
Darkness floods the window's
hollow void.
Impossible to see you.

I scrape the broken shards of glass
and scratch my eyes
Climb through the narrow window
into the wide night.
Alone. Your promise drifts away
upon the moon's cool sigh.
Impossible goodbye.

The jury of stars overhead shape
an unforgiving crowd
above glassy shards of broken hearts
laying shattered on the ground
The fractured wreck of lives lived
too proud (You are gone).
Impossible moves on.

As sunrise splits the sky she wakes
beneath the broken windowpane
She feels her way slowly
through the scattered remains
Stakes the sharpest-toothed shard
as her battle-lost claim

Places it gently in her jar of glass
from broken windows past
The jagged edges dance.
Laugh.
She takes them with her
down an empty path.
One day she will wear them like diamonds

Eleanor Besley

New Faces

I took out my smiles on Tuesday
to wear in the library,

thin days and thinner nights
are no place for fat smiles.

Searching, I found them folded
under layers of tissue.

Behind a sprig of rosemary
I found half a smile,

outgrown by a cousin and
worn one afternoon in Derby

so soft, it masks
the corners of my morning.

Elizabeth Walker

Quiet Grief

I want to make waves
That ripple through the calm
It's so very quiet
And eerily numb

I'd like my skin to tingle
Like butterflies in my palm
It's ever so quiet
But for life's gentle hum

I'll sit here anyhow
In silent echoes
Listen to the quiet
Until its hour of close

The sadness is close
Like calls I've overcome
Grief is so very quiet
Heavy heart a muffled drum

I'll save making waves
For when it's my day
And this weighty quiet
Is ready to give way

Meanwhile on still water
Rest here with me
And enjoy the quiet
Nano flow of calm sea

Sylvie Songbird

The Loss of a Loved One

No anger do I feel
for your premature departure
from this untimely world.
Nor sadness grows still
with every creeping day
that takes me further from you.
No flowers can reflect
the spirit you once contained,
purer than the purist snow,
nor winter breeze remind me of
the lonely heart I steal
from the broken arms of time.
And nay shall I grieve
for this bitter end you did find upon yourself
for time will not depart us now,
fixed as you are in my heart,
nor death can steal your love from me,
that life could not retain.

Julie Missen

Above the Mist

I wish I could fly high above the mist,
up in the clear sky away from the dementia smog,
the mist, the fog that's engulfing my mind.

Dementia's tide of change,
it erodes the shores of my mind,
changing my landscape with every wave.

I build defences to live behind,
strong and stable in my mind.
I must keep building to stem the tide.
But dementia keeps taking my mind.

But I will continue to
build castles out of the rubble of my dementia.

Peter Berry

Unpredictable Dementia

Unpredictable dementia.
Some days I walk tall, straight and strong
And other days I'm weak, bent over and old,
Like living with a wild-eyed horse.
Uncontrollable, unpredictable dementia.
Dementia is my nothing
And my nothing is coming towards me.

Peter Berry

In the Eye of the Dementia Storm

I stand in the eye of my dementia storm,
Trying to focus on the thoughts that circle me.
Faster and faster, they twist.
As I reach out and grab them, they turn to dust and are gone.
And yet I stand in the eye of the dementia storm
Safe and calm and happy.
As always.

Peter Berry

A Poem for a Mute Man

I had to watch Clive drowning in his own eyes,
looking like his yacht had capsized
His raw pain is like a tidal wave again.
Rendered mute by disease,
Clive stands ill at ease
and stares pleadingly
at my hot cup of tea.
He's only allowed a warm beaker.
No sugar – only nasty chemical thickener.
He longs to say loudly:
'Why did I end up this damned way?
I sailed my yacht to Italy.
Now people wash and feed me,
strangers visit who look like me.
People say they're my family.'

Robert Lenney

In My Daydreams

I see you in my daydreams,
You are the butterfly,
That flutters by me,
A little too close.

I see you in my daydreams,
You are the blackbird,
That sings to me,
From the highest branch.

I see you in my daydreams,
You are the gentle breeze,
That plays with my senses,
On a summer's day.

I walk forward,
Every day, getting stronger and taller,
Until I am old,
With you in my daydreams.

Elisabeth Sherriff
From Elisabeth's book In My Daydreams

Goldilocks and the Three Brothers

Big brother - a bit too thin
Little brother - a bit too fat
Middle brother was just right
You can't argue with that fact!

Big brother hides in the background
Little brother stands up proud
Middle brother went his own way
never following the crowd

Big brother gets so stressed
Little brother seems so laid back
Middle brother held my hand
as we walked along the track

Big brother likes perfection
Little brother says "that will do"
Middle brother whispered softly
"Do you know how much I love you?"

Big brother is always working
Little brother loves to play
Middle brother loved us deeply
How I wish he could have stayed...

Sarah Nicholson

The Parasol

Beneath that dazzling, domed Verona sky,
In azure blaze of noon, my mistress stepped.
"To shrift!" she'd told them, with averted eyes,
While on her porcelain skin my shade I stretched.

Into St Peter's Church she flew, to make
A world-without-end promise, hand in his,
Forgetful of me now, for her love's sake,
Unsheltered, rushing onwards to her bliss.

Long hours I waited in a dusty pew:
A witness merely, furled, and stiff, and thin.
I heard the thrum of rain, a beat which grew
To pounding thunder as they carried in

My Juliet, now ghostly-white, returned,
Her pure skin paler now, her lids like lead.
She lay, while all around her, tapers burned,
In shade more deep than I had ever spread.

Richard Spencer

Maybe We'll Rise

Maybe we'll rise
become part of a cloud
in the blue and float over a mountain
Become a tear but not one shed in sorrow
more raindrop then a river running free
Maybe untethered
we'll spring as a fountain
and quench grass in a lush summer lea

Or become part of that glow
forming moonbeams and sunlight
or sail on the invisible breeze
Become the light and the breath
of an Earthly existence and
whisper through valleys and trees

Maybe we'll drift
and be part of the ocean
or dance on the crest of a wave
Or reflect silver on turquoise
twinkle and spark
like ballerinas at dusk in the bay
Maybe we'll graze amongst flora and fauna
or just rest wherever we lay
Maybe we'll rise like a cloud on the mountain
At dawn at the end of the day

Gary Milsom

Our Mothers are Such Safe Harbour

Mum, you were always a safe harbour when needed.
You shielded and protected us and soothed our fears.

Our tears could fill all the seas and oceans.
Instead, we send you abundant love, peace, and light.

A beautiful soul, free from pain has been released into the afterlife.
Walk into the light mum with pride for the family you leave behind.

May you sail gently towards a safe harbour and peace of mind.
Your love lives on in our hearts and will never die.
One day we will see you again on the other side.

Lina Hogg

ECHOES

I can see the echoes everywhere.
A shadow, the way it falls;
The light casting its glow in a room.
Because you once were there.
Somewhere in time is our echo.
The sound of laughter, the look of love;
A smile, a touch, a glance, a kiss.
And all because you once were there.
The echoes hit hard,
Filling me with mourning;
A sadness, and even a despair
All because you are no longer there.
Our echoes go on alone,
Just the memories crossing over,
A thin thread to keep things alive;
For I hope that one day, you will be there.
But for now, our echoes live on,
Yours fading as years go by
Becoming mute, a silent glow;
But I know you once were there.

Samantha Mattocks

OF People & *Places

and

several of Suffolk

Ebb Tide at Stiffkey Salt Marshes

Pot-holed track bumps him to the shore
swaying, swerving, navigating
to a grating halt
the gravel parking place
marked by a wooden post with an oak leaf sign.

Swinging out and rising –
pulls on beanie
khaki cargo pants stretching
stomping hiking boot crunching
cigarette butt stamped but stinking.

He stares at
shingle giving way to low grey-green clumps
sedges, saltwort, and samphire before
making for the path that
slides and winds through twisting
putrescent creek-beds
a trail cross falling wooden bridges
to rippled sand and the waiting
blue green breakers.

Ian Hartley

Aldeburgh

You did him proud Maggi
on Aldeburgh's shingly shores
showing your love and respect
making us reflect
on his genius and yours

Sounds of inspiration
whisper through gigantic shells
your vision added to his
enhancing the stories he tells

He gave us music full of crashing waves
and gentle ripples
mighty storms and quiet sunsets
beauty and melancholy mingled together
in strings and voices

How many pass by without knowing,
walking dogs or just skimming stones
missing out on the glorious message
your art pulls through words from the wind
but lovers of music are pilgrims placing
footsteps on pebbles of dreams

Janet Dunn

63

262

Through leafy Hampstead lanes we run
In dappled late September sun
Aunties Uncles Cousins one
Promised ice-cream promised fun
Joyful laughter free of care
Floats on honeyed Autumn air

But mellow season cannot keep
The hallowed Highgate from their sleep
Where verdant vine and ivy creep
On Marx's tomb the sunbeams leap
While in lengthening shadows deep
Wives and willow softy weep

And there and there and there again
Cardboard shields from fickle rain
Those hopeless souls of no abode
Nomads of the Finchley Road
Scorched from heat and burned from cold
Youthful faces turned to old

As with decaying withered leaves
An emerald Summer Autumn thieves
Floating from the ambered trees
As tumblers on a high trapeze
Clogging gutters filling eaves
Pirouetting on the breeze

And from the Heath in fading light
We skip to race and climb the height
Of steps and stairs
Of chessboard squares
Up to warm and wondrous flat
Where fluffy rug greets scruffy cat

And gazing from my rooftop view
The sunset seen from 262
Symphonically accompanied by
The thrum of traffic rising high
Drifting ever upwards to
The open window painted blue

And lofty voices from the hall
With love and comfort to me call
A family of Queens and Kings
From gaslit hob the kettle sings
Brown sugar cubes
And all these things

Not gone not lost nor cold with frost
But vivid memories gold embossed
Forever wrap around us warm
And weather us from darkest storm
In colours bright to those who knew
The happiness of 262

Karen Turner

Song of Kerkyra (Corfu)

Could any island be more fair
Than this of sweetened Summer air?
Kissed by Zeus and scorched by time
Lie steepened slopes where Cypress climb
And neath the scented olive grove
Glistens shimmering emerald cove
Where mid the mystic pools of green
Mermaids serve Ionian Queen
And to Venetian Citadel
Chimes the white-washed chapel bell
That lingers soft on evening air
Could any island be more fair?

Karen Turner

Battle of Sole Bay 1672

Once, Southwold saw the Battle of Sole Bay
With the Dutch fleet just ten miles from the shore.
But English troops were there on holiday.

The men were busy enjoying their stay
For inns provided fun and ale galore.
Once, Southwold saw the Battle of Sole Bay.

A warning by the French caused great dismay
And news of frigates shook them to the core.
But English troops were there on holiday.

A call to arms was made without delay
By James, the Duke of York, a cry for war.
Once, Southwold saw the Battle of Sole Bay.

Edward Earl of Sandwich in disarray
Was forced to leave his doting paramour.
But English troops were there on holiday.

He sailed the Royal James to the affray
Convinced that he would see his friends no more.
Once, Southwold saw the Battle of Sole Bay.

The warships' guns and flames midst the sea spray
Left thousands dead and injured forty score.
But English troops were there on holiday.

Edward's remains turned up down Harwich way
Known only by the ribbon that he wore.
Once, Southwold saw the Battle of Sole Bay.
But English troops were there on holiday.

Beverley Bowry

3am Shout

Awakened by the bells and light,
heart pounding,
hair standing up and struggling to put my trousers on.
Oh, what a sight!
Sliding down the pole, I hear voices saying, "what we got?"
"Persons reported, come you lot."

Pushing feet into cold boots and leggings,
with tunic zipped I mount the truck.
Blue flashing lights reflecting everywhere,
warning others to beware,
but it's 3am and they should be in bed with any luck!

Turning the corner, an orange glow of flames
leaping from windows comes into view.
I knew I should have gone to the loo!
Those thoughts of wee soon go,
when I hear the screams of a woman,
standing next to a tree.

"My boy, my boy, help him."
Breathing apparatus donned, hoses charged,
"Water on"
and through the door we go,
into a burning hell crawling and keeping low.
"Where are those stairs? We can't have far to go."

Through smoke so thick we feel our way,
passing the lounge or front room as some would say.
A voice inside my head franticly asks, "where is he?"
It's 3am, he should be in bed,
cuddled up to his favourite ted.

Finally, stairs, it's so hot, extremely hot!
Climbing one step at a time,
we must give it our best shot.
Two rooms searched,
in cupboards, on cupboards, behind cupboards,
in bed, on bed and under bed.
"Where is he?

He must be somewhere else instead."
Another door, another room,
"I'm running low on air, we got to find him soon."
"He's there, on the floor."
"I've got him now let's head back to the door."

Down the stairs and into the streets,
where a young mother weeps.
Flowing tears of joy as she cradles her little boy.
Back to the station we go.
Some say we are heroes; you know!
But it's just our job,
even though there can be times when we sob!

Russell Webb

Jen Reid

Jen Reid was the statue that temporarily replaced the one of Richard Coulson after It was toppled in Bristol

That toppling done, this eloquent reply.
Next morning, kids took selfies by her side:
New clench of hands punched peepholes in the sky
As if a stifled voice, now amplified,
Reverberated through the Bristol air.
She looked, her sister gasped, "Just so surreal":
That beacon-fist, that flaming frizz of hair ;
So there she blazed, in resin and in steel,
A surge of power, a rocket, overnight,
That transcendental moment, crystallised,
Refulgent figure, bathed in morning light.
She grinned, her voice enraptured, energized:
"A statement for us all; it's not just his –
That's pretty bloody ballsy, that it is"

Richard Spencer

To Gerald Massey

Minor Victorian Poet!
You Existed! You had your say!
But I never heard your name at school
Nor ever would, until today
Netted sight of your Collected Works
In an obscure rock pool on e-bay.

700 pages of trilling thrust
Clapped with calf-skin, stitched & trussed!
700 sails once filled with gust
Now plunged in sedimentary silt & dust;
Where hold their breath in darkness hid.
I even thought about a bid.
But, having looked you up on Wikipedia
I knew I'd never want to be reading yer!

David Scotford

My Happy Place

we lost the campaign, forced
to leave the historic Spa Gardens
I'm lucky, relocated to a new spot
The Dip, Old Felixstowe

unlock the bright pink doors
unpack my treasures for the new season
sweep the floor, wipe the walls
write on the blackboard welcome 2023

the buxom beach belle is reunited
with the Victorian male bather
Jonathon Livingstone seagull
made by Jacqueline, flies onto his hook

wash black mould from beach hut mugs
tins for tea bags, trays, towels, coasters
all adorned with seaside theme
hang the mirror, with shells by Beryl

painted pebbles and rocks
spots, stripes, starfish, boats
dated memories
2014 Sarah, Mum, Millie, Daniel

pastel striped curtains and cushions
photos of beach days
with Claire and Ellie, Catherine, Brian
sailing boat named Sarah's Happy Hut

big bright boxes of blankets
buckets, balls and spades
life is good at the beach postcard
I do like to be beside the seaside plaque

the lighthouse calendar is on March
the seagull thermometer reads nine degrees
multicoloured beach shoes and towelling robe
wait expectantly for sea swimming days

now it's coats and boots
fleece, gloves and scarf
the kettle whistles
I sip hot tea from a Southwold mug

Sarah Caddick

On the Huh

Grandad put a picture up
You could see it was on the huh
Don't leave it like that
Take a step back
Please straighten that up buh

He stood removed his cap, scratched his head
Looked one way then the other
Looked for a second opinion then
Well what do you think mother?

Gran stood up to take a squint
She stepped from side to side
That looks a rumun
It's on the huh!
I'm sure it's straight he cried

Well why ask my opinion then
All you do is moan
She calmly picked her knitting up
Then sat back on her throne

He took off his cap, turned his head
Gave it another scratch
Looked at the pictures next to it
Too see if they did match

I've looked at it once, I've looked at it twice
It all looks fine to me
Then sat down with a great big sigh
And took a sip of tea

By this time it has to be said
Gran was in a grump
Pop was sulking, moving the corner up and down
They'd really got the hump

So if their house you happen to be passing
And notice a picture on the tilt
Don't say a word I beg you
As you'll add to old pop's guilt

Fred Fish

Crochet Me a Life

Crochet me a life
Crochet me a sign
Crochet me a memory
To show this once was mine.

Four Bury Cottages, Eastwoodbury Lane
The place that held my childhood
Where I cannot come again.

Crochet me a teenager
Looking for her place
Anxious, mixed up, angry
At two, Warner's Bridge Chase.

Crochet me a bride
Living in Park Lane
A tiny Southend attic flat
Our shelter from the rain.

Crochet us a family
Happy as we played
In swanky Earls Hall Avenue
Sixteen years we stayed.

Crochet us an empty house
Children grown and gone
Echoes bounce from silent walls
Time for moving on.

Crochet us in Suffolk
Found where we belong
To sing with friends, to write, to walk
To grow, and to be strong.

Crochet me the signposts
Of the places I have owned
To hold in loving memory
The people I have known.

Sue Thompson
From Sue's book Crochet Me a Life

St Peter's Churchyard on St. Valentine's Day

Remnants of an early morning mist
Settle in bulky wedges
Hovering over the quiet cemetery
Where, newly inscribed tombstones
March solemnly onwards
Followed by generations of those
Who have passed before, on through the gate
Into an unknown, unnamed land

More solid tombs, bare a thick
Coating of moss and twisting
Garlands of waxy, winter ivy
Spring flowers lie in clusters nearby
Settled into a newly warmed ground
Snowdrops and celandines are joined
By brave, brightly-bold, pink cyclamen
Striking out early, in a mild February

The birdsong rises, filling the air
It being St. Valentine's Day
The robin, thrush and blackbird
Are intent on seeking out a partner
Each have their own unique, melodious call
The robin, with its rich soft, almost nostalgic
Drawn-out notes, reminds us of winter's past
While the blackbird, whose song is slow, fluted
Forever changing, while uniquely stylish
And the thrush, sharing a continuous song
With musical, repeated phrases
Which itself, becomes poetic

All three birds, so sure of a future
Promote an optimism
Unfettered by thoughts and hopes
Which extend beyond this fine spring day

Brenda Wells

Orwell

Windows down smoke is out
going forty over the bridge
a quiet memory of an instructor arrives saying
you should never coast in neutral
my foot comes off the clutch

ahead the horizon disappears
the bridge now goes to nowhere
there is the road - on it there are cars
but there is nothing aside from sky and sky
at night there would be stars

I cannot hear the sound of my own voice
over wind over music over the noise of passers-by
in this small old car going forty, still
no one would hear you scream
or sing or cry

my hand is blown back by the bridge-high breeze
the other steady steering with the wheel
breathe in - and the June air is brave
laden with expectation the warmth is here to stay
breathe out - and the temptation here is strong
to close my eyes for just a moment
just a moment too long

then the moment is gone
another impatient in another fancy car wants to get past

the bridge ends and the bottom of the earth returns
I am forced to let this pass

Isabelle Cory

Of Water

A tall mast reflects a long, writhing snake
Which slivers its way, pointing an accusing finger
At clumps of fauna, speared by brittle sticks
Their ends driven deeply into riverbed mud

Seaweed waves it's fat podded limbs
Shimmering, sinewy, twisting on moving water

Abandoned boats, give up their worn hulls
To the mirror of the river, which neatens
Then returns the compliment
Of their images to them

Flooding has left a memory of water
Moving away from its source
To show pristine surroundings
Brickwork and neat doors, which peer out
Through a pebble-strewn, dun-coloured
Liquid surface

Boat shaped moorings, of time-hardened mud
Filled now with water
Await the return of their occupants

There is quiet, there is beauty
The ripple on the surface, gentle
Spring sunshine warms the skin
The air, now soft and mild

But all is temporary
When darkness falls or the water rises
All can change, those living on the river
Know, to be ever watchful

Brenda Wells

Her Gold

They told her there was gold in the Suffolk clay,
She dug with her bare hands but found only their mocking.
They told her there was power, jewels and nobility in the books
and only rag tags and bobtails in the clay.
But she knew the trinity. The Punch, the Red Poll and the ram.
She knew the sunrise, the sunset.
She knew the cow parsley, the milk wort and the wild strawberries.
The right place for the bell heather,
Wood-sorrel and groundsel,
The light and the shade.
The nooks of trees where mistletoe grew that she would weave
with ivy and stud with holly berries like rubies.

She knew skipping home from school.
The books left behind and the sun in her eyes.
Balmy evenings, blackberries sour.
Heady scents carrying over flint, over crinkle crankle walls.

She saw the planes cutting up the sky.
She heard the bells chime in forty six.

A tea cup for her birthday.

The field days in the summer sun.
And so much later, the bright garden mornings,
The pruning and the fruit trees,
Treasures to show the grandchildren, lost speckled
birds' eggs in little boxes
wrapped carefully in cotton wool.
The acorns put in little hands.

She saw and she heard and she held the little hands,
It was love and she knew.

Cheryl Schmidt

And so it was voted unanimously
As no-one was liked by Hetty McGee
'Twas better she stayed where she wouldn't be pestered
By everyday life and those she detested

And without hesitation the hole was filled in
Which slowly but surely diminished the din
The people rejoiced at last they were free
From the poisonous tongue of Hetty McGee

A carnival followed the Mayor gave a Ball
A Conga line started outside the Town Hall
Harmonious peace was quickly restored
(Collective relief down at the Gas Board!)

So now where the hole was along the High Street
The townsfolk have placed a memorial seat
A reminder to all who pause there to rest
A kind word to others is always the best

And keep a sharp eye out for holes on the way
Lest humble pie be your dish of the day
For those who sustain to complain constantly
Should remember the ballad of Hetty McGee!

Karen Turner

The Thicket

Across the field
Stands a dense, stout thicket
Formed over long years
A conspiration of trees
Each leaning heavily
Into its neighbour, cleaving
Keeping its fellows in
Its enemies out
Forming a gang
Drawing up county lines
Strangers are not welcome here

A patch of land, impenetrable to most
Where small creatures, wind their way
Through lower branches
Between tangled, thorny brambles
Which bend, twist and twine
Straggle, snatch, scratch, catch and snag

Darkly within its centre, roots
Are forced deep, into the rich earth
Growth is intense, for brush and bush
As all fight to survive
Where there is shelter for some
Who remain held,
Contained in this shady copse
Hidden from the light
So that saplings and shrubs
Grow stunted, curled, ugly and gnarled

Brenda Wells

The Journey

Atop a hill in Suffolk, a tiny spring bubbles forth water
and descends in trickling runnel.
Joined by narrow brooks, till the sum becomes a stream
which zig-zags to discover slope in that flat land.

Gathering strength, the stream becomes a river
flowing placidly through meadows,
where in summer cattle graze and anglers
pit their wits 'gainst cunning trout and bream.

Ever stronger grows the river,
wider and deeper, till upon its surface boats are bourne.
Now turbulent and excited, it journeys to the sea
as though it hears a distant call and must obey.

On a wind-swept day in March, a different scene
as on its surface and above, the grey of geese,
the white of swans and seagulls' wings,
and cries of seabirds battling in the wind.

 Near at hand, a booming sound,
as relentless tide meets turbulent river current.
Among this troubled power is water from a tiny spring,
which bubbled forth upon a hill in Suffolk.

Muriel Driver

Impressions of Madeira

By Day...
I can't believe how lush it is here
for a rock atop of the ocean
The Sun's beating down
through a breeze warm and gentle
which just keeps the palm tops in motion
You wouldn't say hilly it's sheerer than that
And though it don't have any beaches
an abundance of flora sprouts up from the foothills
getting greener as upward it reaches

An Evening stroll...
Ferns and palms and shapely leaves
a backdrop of all shades of green
to a yellow, mauve and orange scene
of fragrant walls you walk between

Time to go...
Farewell Madeira -You're so very nice
But I'll be back for some more
Now I've tasted a slice

Gary Milsom

Thomas Wolsey, Butcher's Boy

A butcher's boy he rose to serve the Crown,
From Ipswich to become papal legate.
But King Henry brought Thomas Wolsey down.

Of vast ability and high renown,
Pope Clement's choice, and Henry's head of state.
A butcher's boy he rose to serve the Crown.

For fourteen years his greatness did abound,
His failings still a topic of debate.
But King Henry brought Thomas Wolsey down.

He claimed he was no traitor, no one's clown,
To cries of 'treason' from the potentate.
A butcher's boy he rose to serve the Crown.

York Place ransacked and stripped of cap and gown,
He swore he loved the King whate'er his fate.
But King Henry brought Thomas Wolsey down.

Now still he sits o'erseeing his home town,
Bronze eyes cast south toward his college gate.
A butcher's boy he rose to serve the Crown,
But King Henry brought Thomas Wolsey down.

Beverley Bowry

The Slaughden Angel

I met an Angel on Slaughden Beach
plunged from a storm bruised cloud
his feet crashed the sea-wall into dust
and flung shingle to scour the sky

a torrent of wind-feathered spume
battered the air and tore my breath
a voice of gravel rasped in my throat
the kiss of tears burnt my skin.

I met an angel on Slaughden Beach
with the face of a father grown harsh with grief
with the voice of a child shrilling accusations
with the hands of a mother grown cold.

I know there's a debt that must, must be settled
I know there's a price to pay
but I don't know the sum or the coin to use
or the date of the day of reckoning.

I met an angel on Slaughden Beach
who spoke my name in the roar of surf
he whispered an answer that was lost in the howl
of the wind and the waves on the lonely reach.

I met an angel on Slaughden Beach
now he is gone and the air is calm
but far out to sea his shadow is dark
and heaves with the surge of the tide.

Elizabeth Soule

Sailing Through Sandbanks

Ropes slap against bare poles, percussive, plinking.
Yachts wait tall till one slides out, mast slanted,
caught in the cruel currents and contrary pressure
of the overweening wind. You feel the triumph

of the hobby sailor, the way he pushed against the pull,
his mastery of mud and mast and mainsail,
and know that if he keeps the shingle bank behind
his safety is assured. Not so those dredged,

washed to the outer edge. They sailed to flee, survived,
and face another battle at their journey's end.

Cathy Gale

The Honeysuckle and the Rose

In June the hedgerows are decorated
With the pale and pastel blooms
Of the honeysuckle and the rose
Which thread and wind through bushes
Where thorns and brambles hold them in place
Each delicate face peers boldly out
Between rich green leaves
Decked out in shades of gentle pinks and cream
Their perfume and pollen
Draw in fat bodied busy bees
Which glance against fragrant petals
Greedily gorge their fill
Then move on

Brenda Wells

The Willow on the Weir
Long Melford Meadows

What words can I give to the willow on the weir?
Cascading in its green magnificence,
shimmering slender columns, the clerestory
of sunlight, the shadow apse,
foundations' cryptic drift into still mill pool.

A family of pilgrim swans glide past,
elegant as gondolas, on the mill stream,
even their surprising effluent is
a sudden puff of emerald smoke
from a magician's wand, clouding the waters.
Grey parasol webbed feet paddle in
rhythmic leathern energy. The young ones
speckled beige and cream, like pebble banks.

Here we lean on the choir loft of the bridge-edge,
to watch the weir's relentless silver-spiked
downward tumble, the rushing splash
which gives shape to the silence,
and leaves us twice-baptised by beauty.

Catherine Guillemin
First published in poetrywivenhoe, day 294, 2023

Crinkle-crankle Wall

I love the crinkle-crankle's quirkiness,
its quiet economy and hidden strength,
no need for buttresses, for inner stress
holds tight the subtle, undulating length.
From East to West, it's perfectly aligned,
so morning sunlight warms the sheltered side,
fruit ripening along espaliered lines,
resisting sea-winds, carried by the tides.
Een slangenmuur they called it, engineers,
who drained the marshland, freed alluvial soil,
that rich, dense blackness, springing with green spears,
of wheat and barley, from their earthy toil.
Strict calculations laboured to create,
the crinkle-crankle's seeming-natural shape

Catherine Guillemin
First published in Twelve Rivers, Spring issue 2023

A Reply to
"I Wanna be Yours"- (by John Cooper Clarke)

Loud and clear from deepest Ipswich
This is my sincere riposte:
Let me be your double dip-switch:
I would swear - no extra cost -
To keep your 'lecky meter running
Supplement your verbal cunning
Lionize your stunning punning -
Be Vice-Bard, your second-string.

I'm an enterprising fella:
I could be your swig of Soave
Or your multi-pack of Stella
Or your pinging Micro-wa-vay.
Let me be your Mitsubishi
Always strong and never squishy
Not like lucky, minted Rishi
I could be your flash of bling.

Fook, I'll even mind my language
Just to be your Number Two;
Be your cheese and pickle sandwich
Eat-by date now over-due.
You can find in me some solace
I won't sulk like Nadine Dorries
Party, lie and hide, like Boris
I could be your ANYTHING.

Richard Spencer

The Waveney Valley

Constant thread through our life
quietly-spoken and unassuming
a pastoral frame for the everyday
your waters moving seawards
leaving fertile growth behind
Gentle poplars, cow-filled pastures
mill houses and marshy edges
a child's brimming treasure chest
we rode bikes through lost lanes as
round-towered churches stood sentinel
Soft light peels back jaded eyelids
sleepy waters draw us in
we see swans gliding on the surface
damselflies that hypnotise
a perfect valley that sustains us

Sheena McCallum.

OF Love and Friendship

N and Nicer Things

Full-moon Love Poem

I know deep inside that this
semi-happy half-full heart
will be made whole
as a note reflected
from my soul.
Under a glistening full moon
she and I will walk together,
soft bodies
holding hands.
She'll stare into my pale blue sight,
I'll be gleefully lost in room sized reflections;
sunshine smiles as we walk.
And her mouth is a red-ringed temple
supported by ivory towers
with a waterfall laugh
and sea-lapping tongue.

Robert Lenney
From Robert's book Dyslexic Dionysian

Beauty and the Beach

You're as warm as the sunrise adorning the horizon,
as soft as the smooth white sand.
We're looking fondly at each other,
walking hand in hand.

Your arms around me are like rays of sunshine,
made of liquid gold.
I wish it would last forever.
What a treasure to behold!

Hues of sparkling, silver water,
show a reflection of your face.
Your beauty just astounds me,
and sends ripples like fine lace.

We are free to fly as birds,
into an endless sky.
The path is set before us,
from morning until nigh.

As we depart from nature's beauty,
on this St Valentine's Day,
we'll take with us, hearts full of memories.
Only our footprints will stay.

Christine Cacot

You Love Me, I Love You

You love me
she said
as the sea loves the shore
high tide engulfs
low tide leaves me exposed
equinoctial extremes
threaten and desert
the waves caress, she said
disturb
torment
I would have you love me, she said
as the rocks love the pool
encircling, protecting
creating a space
at the edge of the world, she said
as the moon loves the sea
she said, I love you

You love me
as the moon loves the sea
he said
your power
creates the equinoctial surge
high and low
you drive me on
with your darkness
your distances
I am drawn to you, rejected by you
I would have you love me, he said
in a still reach
of calm water
where light kisses the horizon
shimmering from sky to shore
as the sea loves the moon,
I love you he said

Elizabeth Soule

98

Surviving the Stretch

As I lay down my head,
His is just rising from a slumber.
As my moths flutter around a flame,
His birds sing a morning chorus.
As my life commits itself into a boring routine,
He seeks out new adventures everyday

For my beloved is as far from me as possible
On this small planet Earth that is ours.
He is living in his America,
The volcanic rocks testament to our existence.
I mourn his absence, a presence never there –
I go to phone, remembering only too late...

But my beloved and I have been one.
We have laughed till we cried, then sang
And in two years hence, we'll be the same again
Only he'll be my husband,
I, his wife.

Samantha Mattocks

Trinity Sunday

He insists on allowing precisely 18 minutes
so we can slip into a middle pew
exactly as the service starts. Which we do.

I am half-hearted chaperone, a church service
easier than sat silent, mourning in her house.
This rarely visited church a constant all my life.
The petulant teenager in me asks why
but is pleased by my lacklustre singing.
The adult spills tears at the first hymn.

I dry my eyes and focus hard on beauty.
This building, immortalised by Constable
where sunlight splinters through stained glass
and age-old angels watch dust motes dance.
Emmanuel, hosanna, cherubim and seraphim -
where else can my tongue taste those words?

The congregation's kindness kindles tears too.
The tender-stern helpers who escort
the infirm to the communion rail.
The guide dog that sits so quietly. The warm
offerings of peace to those in nearby pews.
I offer a hug, which he will not remember.

Later, on summer lanes that take me home
I relax, breathe deeply and notice
an abundance of poppies everywhere.

Sheena McCallum

I Walked Until I Could Walk No More

I walked and walked on a path less trodden.
I walked searching for I know what,
absorbing the sounds and smells in a blissful trance.
My eyes devoured the beauty of the world around me.
Butterflies, so many butterflies, gentle and graceful.
And I walked, through wind and rain, thunderstorms too.
My ears hear a distant hum of humanity,
but it mattered not as I heard her calling; gentle, strong,
peaceful.
And I walked.
Intoxicated with her radiant love,
I fell into my mother's comforting embrace.
I walked no more.

Lina Hogg

Irish Song

I am a landgirl
And you are the sea
Your tide laps my shore
Taking pieces of me
I want to hold on dear
Through my fingers you slip
And I'm left
Hands and eyes wet

I am a landgirl
And you are the sea
We share the same air
But what of our needs
Mine to hold on dear
And yours to be free
Mine to hold on dear
And yours to be free

Sylvie Songbird

Love

Love cannot be denied by time
Nor held back by tide or season
It cares not for waning moon or solstice
Or the migration of birds or fickle hearts
It cannot be measured or counted
It is infinite as grains of sand
As boundless as sky
It cannot be shackled by chain
Nor governed by King
It is wretched as Winter tempest
Indifferent as Spring
Heady as halcyon Summer
Blithe as slumbery Autumn morn
Sombre as darkening dusk yet optimistic
As a wishful dawn that breaks and brims
With wonder and ambition and promise
Searing soaring silent roaring
Untameable unknowable glowing and unseen
It is the sentinel of the heart
Ever hopeful
Ever faithful
Evergreen

Karen Turner

The Red Sofa

There's a charity shop at the end of my street
with a window display that's so bold
The people who work there are really quite sweet
and the shop it has things to behold

Whilst browsing the floor my eyes were soon led
to some furniture by the far wall
The item in question a sofa bright red,
in the corner with no love at all

I sat on its cushions I sank through the springs
the most comfortable I'd ever been
I then wondered if it could tell me such things
like its history and what it had seen

As I wallowed in comfort I reached at the back
where the cushions don't quite reach the frames
My hand found its way down the tiniest crack
there a postcard containing two names

The card was so faded, had been there for years
the handwriting hard to make out
Its faint smell of lavender moistened by tears
a love token without a doubt

The card was postmarked Dieppe Northern France
a poppy field gracing its cover
It was written to Molly, they'd met at a dance
from Jack her soldier boy lover

As I sat on the sofa I imagined the scene
when Molly had first got the card
The first line read Hi Molly how have you been
and please do not take this too hard

I've been wounded dear Molly, I'm on my way home
I'll soon be beside you my dear
I imagined poor Molly being there all alone
her head filled with heartache and fear

As the red plaid engulfed me I started to well
and my tears soaked the arm of the chair
Did Jack get to Molly away from his Hell
and again run his hands through her hair

And then under the cushion a newspaper clip
dated November nineteen fifteen
It recalled the sinking of a small rescue ship
that was lost and no more to be seen

Had Molly then realised she'd lost poor young Jack
that her love had then perished at sea
Had she known that her young Beau was not coming back
to a life they had both dreamed would be

I looked at my watch it was quarter to four
I'd been lost in a world from the past
I knew that poor Molly and Jack were no more
but I also knew true love does last

Stephen Oakes

105

Hidden Lusts

I see you from afar
I see the way you smile
You haunt my dreams at night
You break my daytime daze
As you catch my wistful gaze
Oh why must we be so?

I dream to feel your touch
I long to know your kiss
You come to me in darkness
When I am not aware
I look but you're not there,
Just an empty night-time room.

I know this must be so
I know it cannot be
And you must never know
How deep my feelings are
Yet in my dreams, we are one
United for all eternity
All I ask is just one night
And a lasting memory.

Samantha Mattocks

A Rondel of Unrequited Fluff

You stretch and yawn and catch me unawares
There's your belly button full of fluff
I reach my finger, but not far enough

I am bereft, can only stop and stare
My heart's like jelly, made from wobbly stuff
You stretch and yawn and catch me unawares
There's your belly button full of fluff

Upon my word you tempt me to despair
My life from this moment on will be tough
I dry my tears upon my silken cuff
You yawn and stretch and catch me unawares
There's your belly button full of fluff
I reach my finger, but not far enough

Sarah Nicholson

The Quarrel

I walked that morning in the nearest place
To country I could find – the local park.
I felt no chill, although the pond was dark
With ice, and as I walked I set my face
Against the February wind. To trace
In memory those last few tender words
You said to me, was bliss and all the birds
Sang descant to my inner song in space.

But love won't stay content and so I asked
You yet again what your desire was.
I did not want to hear the truths you told.
That morning, in the park, I could have basked
In Winter's sun and burned. Night's fire was
A bare hand's breadth away – and I was cold

Joanna Ellis

Mute

The first time I cried
In front of you
I hid in the loo
To begin with

Then I put on my big girl pants
And decided I should speak
I felt ashamed and weak
But I came to find you

I opened my mouth
To explain what I felt
To ask you what you felt
But...... Nothing came out

Only a string of incoherent blubs

The heat in my face rose
Wood fire aflame
Eyes fluttered shut in shame
Search lights scanning for courage

And I couldn't speak
You sighed
I just cried
Uncontrollably
Wrapped round you for comfort
Empty

Sylvie Songbird

Talking About Old Friends

Where are your old friends my 'friend'?
You know, the ones you have known for years.
With whom you share your tears.
The one who is always there,
who will always care,
and listen to your fears ...

Who knows who, what, and why.
And with whom you're not shy.
The friends with shared memories
of you, of your loved ones.
Who have seen you uncovered, unwrapped!
Who have laughed with you,
cried with you... might even
have died with you!

Who have shared the odd trip with you.
Slept in a tent with you,
even a bed ...
maybe - your shed!
It's someone, at some-time,
with whom you've 'gone on ahead'.

Laughed 'til you cried.
Drunk more than you should
- before getting to pud!
Who remembers your life,
your trouble and strife.

Because they are the ones
who – as life rumbles on
will be there and be strong
... when you can't carry on.
When you desperately need help,
and it all feels wrong,
they'll be there 'with a song'.
To scoop up your heart,
which they've known 'from the start'.

These friends are the ones
who care for you – all.
And cherish your soul.
A mutual respect, a kindness;
a 'mindness'; a timelessness.
Value them dearly,
protect them fearlessly;
they're priceless.

Jane Spencer- Rolfe

A Mother's Love

Her journey flies by
with a blink of an eye
She tries hard to slow it
Runs alongside them
but they just keep on moving
till it's time for goodbyes

The ties of her aprons had to be cut
and the small hand in hers
is now just a dot
in the depths of her memory
where she keeps them all hidden
And the chatter that filled
the very air that she breathed
Replaced with a silence
in which she feels grief
for the laughter, the chaos, the fun.

The house had energy,
and heaved from the strain
from days filled with parties
and play when it rained
They built dens in cupboards
and under the stairs
and buses from cardboard
with cushions for chairs
Cabbages and carrots
made from salt dough
and paint filled a small shop
where an eager child
waits to pay for their goods
in a small paper bag
with imaginary money
they thought they once had

She sits by the window
and pictures them playing
shouting words

of encouragement
and praising them, saying,
'How clever you are; keep on pedalling,
my darlings'

But the past is the past
and the toys now lay idle
and the chatter from children
is her song with the title,
 'A love song for mothers
from children she loved.'

Placing boxes on shelves,
she sees smiling faces
from days by the sea
and squeals of excitement
Precious memories to treasure of days
on the sand with buckets and spades
tightly held in their hands

Drawings and objects
with dabs of red paint
they hand them all over
with smiles as they wait
for praise from their mother,
who quickly replies,
'You are so clever!'

To a mother, it's never
a chore but a joy
of life's little pleasures,
from her girl and the boys

To have and hold for times in the future,
she will open the box as a mother, a tutor
Her thoughts will go back
to a house full of laughter
and days of deep joy
when they called her their mother.

Belinda Rose Bond

OF Trolleys Drowned & Stranger Things

OR Setting Straight The Record

The Ghost

I want to stay here,
here in a world that is not mine,
I want to touch faces I cannot touch
and mingle amongst the ones that I love,
to know that I am alive and to see your pain
wrapped cold in your vicious lies;
that tore my consciousness from soul
and stole the world from my eyes;
that crusted and wounded cannot speak
of the visions that now I see;
your laughter that is filling this house
where once I was wandering;
your sorrow child that is buried deep
within the rotting carcass of me;
that weeps still for the every day
that you have stolen from me.
And never more shall my soul rest
whilst yours is living still,
but shatters, silent in my cold world
that suffers from your kill.

Julie Missen

The Adulteree

What are you? Are you a big man now? Now you have pulled down the castle we toiled to create. The years of sacrifice and commitment to our joint future, dissolved in your childish fancy.

You sucked the soul from me. All I did was try to love you. My body is scarred where our child lay and fed. Yet she will cry at your malice. Your pursuit of sin will ripple and echo around her life forever.

What about me? I'll cry over you. But I shall not remain bitter. I'll mend my broken heart and I'll love again. But you, your guilt and regret will haunt you forever.

Christopher P. Stapleton

An Afternoon Walk

It is after midday,
And, filled with wine and warm food,
We flatten the wet grass
With clumsy trudge.
Leaves reveal the sun's prismatic flashes,
Intermittent arrows that offer
Blind comfort.

The damp air smells of twilight,
Though the day's hardly done.
And each stone, weather-worn,
Deflects a close inspection,
In shades of shadowy blue.

We tiptoe around the grassy mounds,
I, imagining the shivering rows, turning,
Where we step,
Disturbed.

We hold hands, but I am
Not there.
I think I hear ancient hymns drift and catch
On the breeze,
And whispered voices slip from slumber,
Diffuse across time, without words.

All that remains is a feeling.
The chipped and crumbling stone fragments;
My thoughts dissemble into shards
On the grass.

And I am in this earth-
This soft, brown, enveloping ground,
Absorbed,
Where no light or sound
Can reach me.

This strange, bleak and hollow silence,
Surrounds me fold on fold,
Where no bird sings,
And stories never told
Fight to surface.

Virginia Betts
From Virginia's book Tourist to the Sun

Skins

We have appropriated many skins

layered skin on skin
to survive the encroaching ice.
We have crucified skins
stretched and tormented them
to shapes quite other
for our own purposes
coracles
bottles
bags.
We are shod in borrowed skin.

We have invented terrible ways
to tenderise
to tan
render supple;
we have chewed and scraped
steeped and stewed and seared and smeared
and peeled
and sliced.
We have tattooed pale translucent slivers
with our myths.

We have stolen many skins
to save our own.

Elizabeth Soule

Architect or Butcher

I am walking in death,
coasting through the world unseen
The pain of my mind, twisting, stabbing,
pushing against my reason
Desperate to discharge evil from my body
to eject the demons through my skin
I trace the ley lines on my arm,
the souvenirs of previous release

I cut deep, the expulsion of pain cathartic, sanguine
I follow the trickle of tears diluting my blood
My flesh is exposed, unlike my soul, hidden from view.
Now I live, now I feel
Still incomplete,
the first cut not the deepest, I gouge further inside

Scoring and grinding I tear at the flesh,
my muscle and bone join in the purge
But, I just float along, alone and unheard
If you could listen to me speak
Maybe you will hear what I say
Please don't try to fix me I just need your ears

Christopher P. Stapleton

Shallow Grave in the River Gipping

Reeds, sharper than knives
fail to conceal
a fifty year old Finefare trolley
sunk to rust like a relic from another age;
insinuating hundreds of ordinary lives;
passing through a thousand pairs of busy hands;
carrying counter-sliced cheese
and tins of spam.
Before Marathons were Snickers,
and Spangles and Space-Dust littered the land.

To end here.
Unceremoniously dumped
by a couple of smacked-up punks
one night after a shopping spree
fifty years ago;
when I pushed him, and he pushed me,
just for a laugh,
and everything was free.

And seeing it rusting there,
its bones protruding, stark and bare
from that stagnant pool of filth,
I wonder what became of him;
and if he, too
took the undignified slide into oblivion,
half-sunk in a shallow grave;
all that shining kinetic potential arrested;
dulled, and silenced
by time.

Virginia Betts

Animals

Take, take and not give
He curls his face into an expression of malice
Twisting and snarling, spittle flying and dripping
Orders, rules instructions, do it or die

No weakness, no sympathy
Bleed them dry of all they have
Take it all suck the marrow from their core
They die, we live we take on the next

Don't breathe with our victims
No mercy for our hopeless quarry
Bite their hamstrings and tear out their hearts
What they had will then be ours

Incredulous I laugh at him
As evil oozes from his mouth like a pus ridden wound
I won't be your patsy, I won't hunt down your prey
Go hunt on your own I need to live

Christopher P. Stapleton

Anne Boleyn

Green was never my colour.
Red – the colour of my dress that day.
Red – the dying light in the sky.
Red – the blood at the birth of my children.
Red – the sword so quickly brought down.

Henry – most famous king of England,
how proud you would be of that.

But famous for what?
For being fat and gaudy,
a jester too clownish to be cruel.

I'd rather be a witch than a fool.

And what came after, dear husband of mine?
Your son died too young
and soon was forgotten.

Our daughter, my daughter,
she's the one who survived
and ruled far better,
far longer than you.

Greensleeves – an idle song for an idle man.

Here is Elizabeth, my child.
Red hair still blazing.

Mai Black
From Mai's book Thirty Angry Ghosts

124

The Dragon Queen

The dragons are a-slumbering in the dragon realm
Dreaming of their queen and when she will return
But Rhodri, king of the dragons
Waits patiently at the gate
For he will never sleep until his queen awakes

The dragon queen is a-slumbering
Outside the dragon realm
In a high-rise building
She toils every day
She's forgotten all the dragons with whom she used to play

She hears the dragons calling her
From within their dragon dreams
She remembers the mountains
Living the dragon way
Making Daisy chains and Sleeping in the hay

The queen's heart is a-beating in time with her dragon kin
And she knows she will return
To a place where time stands still
Her realm she will restore
Then the dragons will be a-slumbering no more

Mandy Simmonds

Accused

For that I knowe the Goodnesse of Herbes
for that I use the Knowledge of Herbes
of the Power of the Moone
of the Secrets of Heartes
to the Goode of Neighboures and their Beastes

for that there are jealouse Souls
who feare my Knowledge
resent my Power
and would laye Blame for their own Faultes
at my Doore

for that the Crueltie of youre Heartes
dictates the Crueltie of youre Handes
I knowe
that by Water, by Rope or by Fire
you will take from me the Breath
of my Bodye.

Your Hatred returneth me
to the Rootes of Oure Being
by Earthe, Aire, Fire, and Water
you carrye the Guilte of my Deathe

my Bodye belongs to the Earthe
Water is my Bloode
Aire is my Breath
my Spirit is Fire
and it burns
for Vengeance.

Elizabeth Soule

Selkie Song

Come my love, oh come to me
From the deepness of the sea,
Never more let parting be
Between thy heart and mine.

I remember well that day
Just before the sun was setting
Saw you standing on the jetty
Dressed in cloak of grey.
I never asked your home or name,
Never questioned why or wherefore,
I knew without a doubt or care
For our hearts beat the same.

There was never any need
To ask or give, let or permission;
Sea and land made intercession,
Nurtured well the seed.
Bonds were made and they hold fast
Through the turns of tide and season.
Though we know not yet the reason
We'll come home at last.

Come my love, oh come to me
From the deepness of the sea,
Never more let parting be
Between thy heart and mine

Joanna Ellis

127

William Shakespeare

You idle-headed clotpoles,
you beslubbering baggages,
you mewling malt-worms.
Is it my fault you don't get it,
you jolt-headed maggots?

I wasn't writing it for you.
I am not the one who troubles
your rump-fed brains.
Direct your wrath more justly.

Still I hear whispers
from the back of the classroom,
from the theatre auditorium,
from the upmarket cinema:
Why didn't he use proper English?
Why is he so boring?
Why is he so dull?

Day and night,
your two loutish thumbs
jab out such beetle-headed bragging,
such dog-hearted lies.
You say you're on fleek,
you slay it,
you shade me.

But you're too nauseating to be sick,
you're wet
and you're thirsty.

I am Shakespeare.
I am The Bard.

I'm fire, I'm flaming,
I'm peng with a quill pen,
no cap.

That's rap.

Mai Black
From Mai's book Thirty Angry Ghosts

Ariadne's Thread

A thread,
I spun a thread for you
and as you plunged into the dark
I looped it round my heart
tethering you
to the light.

I felt each twitch and tug
as you trod deeper
into the labyrinth.
Each twist and tug
tore a little
from somewhere deep in me

but even worse were my imaginings
when, for a time, the thread went slack.
What struggles were unfolding
far from the light,
what battles fought,
what wounding?

And then the steady, rhythmic
twist and tug
as you rewound the skein,
came back to me.
I thought that was the end
the happy end

but somewhere since
the thread between us has
unravelled,
you let it drop
and now I drift
untethered.

Elizabeth Soule

Samhain

Tonight the veil is at its thinnest,
our ancestors are closest,
whispering in our ears,
pleading to all our fears.
We need to listen and learn,
to their wisdom we yearn.
We should retune our ears
(abandoning our fleeting fears)
to their tales in the winds
to calm our hearts' wild minds.

Robert Lenney

The Ballad of Hetty McGee

Miss Hetty McGee, a cantankerous soul
Had the misfortune to fall down a hole
Caused by a gas leak 'neath the High Street
Found itself in the path of Miss McGee's feet

From below Miss McGee was heard to exclaim
'This is outrageous I wish to complain!'
But having complained for sixty-four years
Miss McGee's woes now fell on deaf ears

And instead of folk leaping to rush to her aid
They pondered her plight and the problem was weighed
For a rescue attempt on Hetty McGee
Spelled infinite grief with a capital 'G'

More moaning and groaning more nasty retorts
More snarling and sniping more formal reports
So should they consider just leaving her there?
Would anyone miss her? Would anyone care?

A lifetime of spite metaphorically speaking
Found Hetty at sea in a boat that was leaking
But instead of relenting and being polite
She continued to rant long into the night

Those she'd belittled those she'd berated
Those who'd been trodden on those who'd been hated
Those she had picked on day after day
Those who'd been silenced now had their say

OF
Philosophy
& Life,
War & Peace
Or
just Daily
Observations

A Revelation at Lunch

sharing dips and ideas
laughing amongst the olives
anticipation with cheese and grapes
chatting as glass half full friends

looking at photos
on your phone
heads touching, leaning in
I smell your skin

with each word you utter
I become more entranced
our perspectives blend
I want to know you

an elephant joins us at the table
invisible to me
deep in my flirting fantasy
have I lost my touch?

you talk of a sleazy weekend in Berlin
still I don't get it
friends dragging you round gay bars
I'm oblivious to the creature until

in disbelief I hear
you say you're gay
my face reddens and
the elephant appears in full colour –

Sarah Caddick

Vernal

It feels like Spring will never bud;
The blossom, trapped, cannot escape
This blue and yellow stained with blood.
It feels like Spring will never bud
While every day the missiles thud,
And mouths, all round the planet, gape.
It feels like Spring will never bud
Until the blossom can escape.

Richard Spencer
- Russia's invasion of Ukraine

Motto

To ride on tiptoe upon the moment,
surfing like some perilous dancer
on the sensation with all dear care
not to ponder with malingering motion
but seize the minute minute and
wrap around the canvas of the day,
embellish yourself with brush-stroke
in suspended animation,
envelop the sundry emotion
for there is strength in cutting out
your heart for the mob's football.

Robert Lenney
From Robert's book Heretic

The Truth of Tides

Today I learned
the truth of tides.
For all its fearful roaring
and ice-white summits
the sea remains constant,
cradled by the gravity
of the sun and moon.
Tides are illusionary.
It is the land which moves.

And we, poor creatures
are hurried, restless,
round and round,
anchored by unwilling motion.
Wondering why
we are now melancholic
now ecstatic
now contended
and now feel such desolation
that we almost cease to be.

And yet there is a remedy,
for standing here
upon the shoreline
looking out upon
that pale blue horizon,
I recall that other self,
the one who knows
perfect stillness,
perfect calm,
the one who understands
the truth of tides.

Mai Black

Tourist to the Sun

Fired-up for take-off,
wearing my asbestos suit, designed to deflect,
I bring with me a cabin full of un-marked
baggage for the hold.

Wing walker without a rope,
hurtling to the light fantastic,
untethered.

First to sign up
to step off the map;
where even the silvery surface is marked by dark spots;
even the brightest star is already dead.

With outstretched arms I
surrender to the sun,
glide, star-shaped, licked by flicking tongues of flame,
into the white-hot core;
white heat devouring sound,
eclipsing time,
searing conscience and
annihilating thought.

Not arrogance that brings me here,
but fear.
The elemental need to fly, unfettered,
to pilot my own craft;
to pierce reality,
and seek the truth behind it,
and, in seeking, half expect to find it.

And thus, avoiding bird-strikes,
negotiate safe water-landings
when at last I am earthbound;
within my hand,
a brand to fire my piece of earth's story

when I return
scorched and burned.

Virginia Betts
From Virginia's book Tourist to the Sun

141

I Felt His Gaze

I felt his eyes following my every move.
What was he looking at, me or my groove?
I pretend not to notice him.
But how could I not, when he's easy to spot?
He is perfection personified.
Those twinkling blue eyes, dark hair
And not a single hair dyed
I sighed!

A bit young for me, perhaps
But then, I'm a young 40 something year old,
With fine abs and no folds.

I drank some more for Dutch courage.
I danced some more too
That's what 40 something year old's do

My heart pounding, I finally approached him
"Hi, do I know you? I mean, have we met before?"
How lame was that?

"Well, actually" He even sounded gorgeous
"I was with your son, at uni. We met at graduation."
I had no salvation, my humiliation complete
Oh, my foolish heart, I better take a seat.

Lina Hogg

Wishing

Put me on a boat at sea
a tiny boat painted red,

with sails up into the sky
to catch the wind buffeting.

On the voyage show me taipans
and floating markets,

make me sail on
into the tiger's eye until

as the storm passes,
I am invisible as salt air.

If the wind changes course
and your flotilla sinks,

let me throw you a buoy
let me sail on.

Elizabeth Walker

Lover's End

She looked in the mirror with tears of despair
The sexy young woman was no longer there
She thought of the men, the fun, and the laughter
She always knew what they were after
Then she met HIM, but it was too late
The years her looks had begun to take
He never noticed her, left on the shelf
And she knew he often made love to himself
She hinted at romance outside of the bed
In the car, on the beach, in his grubby old shed
He surprised her by saying he'd like it now and hot
But he meant apple crumble, the ignorant clot
So, she packed all her stockings away in a box
And tried to find fun in knitting socks
For charities of which she was now one
Her time as a lover was finally done

Mandy Simmonds

The U15's Manager

Man on! Get it away!
testosterone surges
dig in deep Harleston Town
who's marking number nine?

Freddie! Jamie! Ethan!
sturdy, leggy half-men
rampant shoulder barging
who's swearing at the ref?

Almighty Christ Harleston!
a freak goal lands in net
they're asleep at the wheel
who's gonna take the blame?

You're pi**ing me right off
weathered arteries pop
black gaffer coat pulled tight
who's bleating all the time?

Come on, we can do this
team captain call to arms
his nervous look at bench
Winners boys - we're winners

Sheena McCallum

A New Year's ... Revolution?

My new broom, has no bristles
Clean sweeps it will not do
Just old stubble,
so I'm in trouble,
when it come to that:
... NEW YOU!
It does though, have an upside
It's raw, it's bold - exposed!
It shows me what I'm
made of - and I think I'm
... 'one of those'!
WHAT is 'one of those'? they cried
S/he didn't say a word
For me to know, and you to see
But why not try – come - follow me.

A New Year's REVOLUTION!
It can't be a 'new you'
So
Are you going to run away?
Or face your life anew?

Jane Spencer-Rolfe

Have You Ever Seen a Candy Floss?

Have you ever seen a sausage roll
a Swiss roll
an apple crumble
an apple turn over
a milk shake
a chocolate flake
a Viennese whirl
or a candy floss?
Have you ever seen a hot dog
a chilly chilli
a shy coconut
a bean run
a potato do the mashed potato
a potato in a jacket
a broad bean abroad
or a soldier in an egg?

Have you ever been to sea in a gravy boat
counted the fingers on a fish
wrapped a pig in a blanket
or found a toad in a hole?

Have you ever heard a jam tart fart?

Elisabeth Sherriff
From Elisabeth's book Bits in the Jam

D.I.Y

Often she would laugh:
"You've such an expressive face!"
And once, more seriously:
"My whole life over
Never have I ever
Known anybody's body
Show a more expressive face on it than yours."
As usual, I replied silently
Somewhat warily, if the truth be told
And conjured up a slippery flicker
Of my quizzical brow
Chasing apologetic dimples.
Last time I saw her was in B&Q.
A slow check out queue held us both, suspended.
She grinned with the unexpected, arid warmth
Of an oven door opened on the Sunday roast.
"I'm here to buy a drill!" she gushed.
Her eyes burnt into me like an arc-welder.
"A phallic symbol? Sure – I know!
That's why I need a big one!
But - I also need to put up some big shelves!"
She went on to joke about a max-torque strap-on
For her Torture Garden tool belt
As if we weren't surrounded
- "I'm in dyke heaven!" -
By elderly men clutching shed paint.

Some months later, when I heard she'd been found
Slumped to her knees
Head on her lap
Alone in her flat
Dead already for several weeks
Like a vulgar wizened hedgehog
The expressions this image drew
Upon my face
To think of her
A walnut shell of rigor mortis
Prayerfully curled like hunchback roadkill
Would have cracked her such a grin
She'd have killed herself laughing
If her own artful wish
Had not beaten me.
At her funeral
Was a professional mourner, paid for by her mother.
So crisply starched
His clothes so black
To look at him swapped your eyes for coal
And he fanned away the sunshine
With a crow's wing in his hat.
And he sang so long & loud & proud
The pews all creaked
Till the church might fall
And the rest of us cowered in mumbles.

David Scotford

149

Music to My Ears

I play a banjo
But not a guitar.
They are too heavy
And the strings stretch too far.

I love my ukulele
As It looks kind of cute.
But I couldn't face a double bass,
Or puff enough for a flute.

My bodhran Is a pleasure
To stroke with a brush.
And my dulcimer's heady notes
Give me a rush.

But it's my thimble-tapping washboard
That gets my main vote of approval,
As it's great for music making
And stubborn stain removal.

Beverley Bowry

Tale of a Trotter

I saw a pig's trotter all covered in chocolate
in a shop window alongside the soap.
It was in a gold box all tied up with blue ribbon
and priced eighty pounds, so I hadn't a hope
of raising the money to pay for this trifle,
no, wasn't a trifle, t'was trotter of pig.
but as I was gazing enraptured with longing
along came an old man with feet rather big.
He placed his large footies in over the threshold
and spoke with his voice to the shopkeeper there
"Oh here's eighty pounds for your chocolate pig's trotter,
please wrap it and send it to Manchester Square".
He stepped from the shop, and then raising a large
stick of rhubarb he hailed an old taxi and left.
with the trotter of chocolate removed from the window
I suddenly felt rather sad and bereft;
For I'd seen it first and although t'was expensive
I knew I could give it more love than the gent
with the feet rather big, and the large stick of rhubarb
so I purchased to cheer me a bottle of scent.
But I'll never forget my chocolate pig's trotter
all tied with blue ribbon in casket of gold,
and I'll never forget the large stick of rhubarb
or the feet rather big of the man, very old.

Joanna Ellis

Shoes

I can't wear stilettos, I find it hard to wear heels,
My toes don't like pinching or tight-fitting styles,
My wellies are useful to put on in the rain,
Walking boots, my saviour, to pull on again.
Love my flip-flops and sandals too,
Lots of colours, grey, pink and blue,
Baseball shoes, long laces, easy to wear,
Trainers for cycling and exercise to share.
Thanks to you all for letting us know
What you like to wear when you've somewhere to go!

Susan Seston

Midsummer's Dawn

I sat with friends on England's sharpest point,
caught between man and
Nature's brightest fires
on our longest day.
To see other mortals folly of
hard tarmac weakened by weeds.
For a short term gain -
We all pay a steep price.
Our future is assured
due to our abuse.
This hearth of the universe,
our beautiful battered home
will outlive us-
But will we survive ourselves?

Robert Lenney
From Robert's book Dyslexic Dionysian

Shadows

Dementia shadows are often long and
dark at the end of a bright day.
A weary mind is a slow mind.
Hopefully tomorrow shall be bright and
clear and dementia's shadows will be
short and light.
From the dark shadow of my dementia
there is light and hope for others.
The beacon in my mind does not always
shine on an empty waste land,
it shines on new growth like a fire-stricken
forest coming back to life.

Peter Berry

Sometimes My Clothes Feel Itchy

Sometimes my clothes feel itchy,
My tee-shirt is far too tight,
My shoes are just too ouchy,
And my PJs don't feel right.

Sometimes my clothes feel itchy,
My sleeves feel far too long,
My trousers pinch my bottom,
And my pants just feel all wrong.

Elisabeth Sherriff
From Elisabeth's book
Don't Let the Peas Touch the Mash

Plum and Apple Jam
France, the trenches, 1915

Cranking open a can of Tickler's plum and apple jam,
Jack closed his eyes and dreamt
of the green smell of apples
on his Dad's allotment,
of the damp, dark earth, and golden plums,
Warwickshire Droopers, hanging
like lanterns in the dusk.

He spread the sticky mixture, turnips and sugar,
on hard biscuits, gulped it down,

Take a Tickler's can and wad with gun cotton,
scrap metal and a simple fuse,
light it with a Lucifer or fag
and lob across the gaping gulf of
No Man's Land.

Jack kept one back, inside the trench, an empty can,
to fill with water and wildflowers:
larkspur, toadflax, and meadowsweet, perhaps
(he wasn't sure of names,
just dandelion, or ' chimney sweeper,' pis-en-lit,
they say in French),
flowers which knew no bounds,
or gas attacks, or hand grenades,
or hands blown off
when reaching out to gather them.

Catherine Guillemin
First published in poetrywivenhoe, day 251, 2023

The Owl and the Pussy-Cat in Lockdown

"This lockdown sh*t...we've waited WAY too long",
To Owl, on Insta, wrote his feline friend,
"I know this place, with trees called things like Bong?
Bring cash + honey, yeah ? It's bang on-trend.
I've hired this well-sick boat, it's like pea-green?
Oh SH*T! We haven't got a frickin' ring!
And don't forget, yeah, give your wings a clean...?"
Unfazed, it seems, by total lack of bling,
They bartered for the piercing of a pig;
A hill-side turkey heard the vows 'n' stuff,
And though their wedding breakfast wasn't big,
That quince and meat and sh*t was well enough.
By moon-light, social distanced-ly, they twerked;
Somewhat against the odds, it kind of worked.

Richard Spencer

Masking

We meet in the street;
you fancy a chat,
and you go on and on
about this,
and that;
I admire your coat;
you admire mine;
I say you seem tired;
you say you'd look better
if you'd had the time,
this morning,
to put your face on.

To put your face on
means make-up;
like after a fight;
so maybe a brave face;
which is war-paint;
which then leads to Braveheart,
smeared and daubed,
leading the charge;
so, leads charging;
well, there's my laptop
at home, charging up,
like a knight on a white horse-
or loitering alone-
like the one in Keats' poem,
where things wither by the lake;
which leads to monsters of the deep,
though technically that's a loch,
like in a door,
without a key;

158

stop, stop, stop!

A quay!
where War-Brides stand
to wave goodbye to their sweet heartland-
and your remark makes my thoughts take off;
spill into my brain
in split-second time,
and, as they take flight,
I miss your next lines.

So, I just keep quiet,
and nod and smile
in the right place, I hope;
put on a made-up face;
wear normality like a cloak;

play out the elaborate spectacle
of the mask,
while behind the crafted veneer,
bottomless wells of thoughts
spiral down endlessly,
and the grey shadow of fatigue
follows fast.

Virginia Betts
From Virginia's book Tourist to the Sun

List of Authors

List of Authors

List of Authors

List of Authors

List of Authors

List of Authors